Francisco Urondo

Fuel and Fire

Selected Poems 1956–1976
Translated by Julia Leverone

DIÁLOGOS
BOOKS

Fuel and Fire: Selected Poems 1956–76
by Francisco Urondo
Translated and Edited by Julia Leverone
Selected from from *Obra poética*,
(Adriana Hidalgo, Buenos Aires 2006).

Work published within the framework "Sur" Translation Support Program
of the Ministry of Foreign Affairs and Worship of the Argentine Republic
Obra editada en el marco del Programa "Sur" de Apoyo a las Traducciones
del Ministerio de Relaciones Exteriores y Culto de la República Argentina

Printed in the U.S.A.
First Printing
10 9 8 7 6 5 4 3 2 1   18 19 20 21 22 23

Cover art: "Círculo vicioso" by Luis Felipe Noé
Book and Cover design: Bill Lavender

Library of Congress Control Number: 2018956960
Urondo, Francisco
Fuel and Fire: Selected Poems 1956–76 / Francisco Urondo
with Julia Leverone, translator and editor
p. cm.
ISBN: 978-1-944884-54-3

DIÁLOGOS BOOKS
DIALOGOSBOOKS.COM

Publications

"For Solitudes" in *American Literary Review*;

"Large, Calm Eyes," "I Cannot Complain," "Days Come and Gone," and "The Tree of Life" in *Asymptote*;

"The Setting of the Planets" in *Beltway Poetry*;

"Loving Her Is Difficult" in *Blue Lyra Review*;

"The Plain Truth" in *Boston Review*;

"Encoded Message," "The Grandson of God," "Milonga of the Marginalized Paranoid," "Nocturnal Fire," "Canons," "Body of Crime," and "Solicited" in the *Brooklyn Rail*;

"Today, a Hearing" in *Interim*;

"Kindness" in *The Massachusetts Review*;

"Mischievous" and "Escola do Samba" in *Modern Poetry in Translation*;

"Shadows for Seeing" in *Poetry International*;

"The Wallet Maker," "Bar 'La Calesita,'" and "Little Heart" in *Storyscape*;

"Mosquitoes" and "Fuel and Fire" in *Tupelo Quarterly*;

"Thank You Very Much" and "Felipe Vallese" in *Waxwing*;

"Goodbyes" in *Witness Magazine*.

.

Índice

Contents

Translator's Note

To combine militancy and artistry—projects of two ethics—can be seen as a conflicted imperative. Yet in the 20th century, poets across the world undertook the task with urgency: in concert, and in response to their times, they changed the poetic line via acts of denouncing, proving, and of making manifest and testament their difficult particularities of war and political and social repression. Think of Wilfred Owen, Yiannis Ritsos, Paul Celan, Zbigniew Herbert, Langston Hughes, Audre Lorde, and Adrienne Rich. Francisco "Paco" Urondo is part of this tradition of pressing the language of a poem to speak, against oblivion, against doubt. And he opened himself into the writing; given his cognizant and representative voice, sometimes daring, sometimes resigned, we know that fighting and art were one for him.

Paco, along with numerous other poets not just from Argentina—Juan Gelman, Mario Benedetti, Ernesto Cardenal, Raúl Zurita, Roque Dalton, Jorge Adoum, Roberto Fernández Retamar, Javier Heraud, Enrique Lihn, and many more, across Latin America and exiled, imprisoned and killed, made to live clandestinely or otherwise harmed—all sustained their positions as artists and activists and intellectuals at great risk while they fought to write with witness against the violent destruction and silence that formed a widespread reality, especially in the 1970s, in the region. Integral to this committed, conversational poetics, and arguably to the contemporaneous poetry of witness abroad, was a positioning of the poet within the poems as a representative addressing an individual reader on an intimate level, frankly and empathetically. This address, in turn, begged of the reader action, beginning with knowledge of the deadly socio-political circumstances.

—

I have been stricken with the direct and accessible; self-effacing and humorous; urgent and raging; and melancholy textures of Paco's Spanish words as they convert to English, as well as with the truths told across them. Wherever I could, I made choices for sound that echo his own internal rhymes and pacing. I preserved the vast majority of his line breaks and punctuation—even when technically incorrect in either language, which conveys a pulsing forward. Paco's voice and message were always on my mind. And they carried away from the translation; in my own poetry, they stay with me. His is a poetics that we can hear clearly in our USAmerican contemporary moment; that is necessary to hear; and that we can still learn from and come to utilize, half a century later.

This is a selection of Paco's poetic work beginning with *Historia Antigua* (Ancient History), 1956 and ending with *Cuentos de batalla* (Battle Stories), 1976, his last published collection. *Fuel and Fire* traces the trajectory of his revolutionary poetry and voice, as these built in response to his nation and region that fell around him.

Introduction by Hernán Fontanet

On June 1976, a few months after the bloody military coup[1] in Argentina that was to result in seven years of brutal military rule and state-sponsored terror, a remarkable intellectual and inexperienced guerrilla fighter was sent to the city of Mendoza. His name was Francisco "Paco" Urondo (1930 – 1976) and his mission was to strengthen the resistance with what in the 1970s was considered one of the most powerful guerrilla organizations in Latin America: the Montoneros.[2] A few days after his arrival, Urondo would be killed, and his name added to a list, according to poet Mario Benedetti, of "no less than 30 poets in Latin America who paid for their commitment to the revolution with their lives."[3]

By 1976, Urondo had already gained significant recognition. He had been widely published. More than ten of his books of poetry, an essay, a novel, two compilations of short stories, and an anthology of Argentine poems were all in print. He had three of his plays staged, had written television, movie scripts and lyrics for songs, and had become a well-recognized journalist who had contributed to numerous newspapers and magazines, including *Clarín* (1967),

---

1 The military coup, which overthrew the unstable democratic government of María Estela "Isabel" Martínez de Perón on March 24, 1976, and established the de facto National Reorganization Process (1976 – 1983) was led by former military officers Jorge Rafael Videla, Emilio Eduardo Massera, and Orlando Ramón Agosti. All have been convicted of human rights violations, including murder, torture, and illegal deprivation of freedom, and sentenced to life imprisonment and loss of military rank.

2 The initial goals of the Montoneros were to secure the return to power of the then-exiled former president Juan Domingo Perón and the establishment of a political system in Argentina they called *Socialismo Nacional*, which they regarded as the natural historical evolution of Peronism.

3 Mario Benedetti. "Paco Urondo: constructor de optimismos." *Poemas de Francisco Urondo*. Madrid: Visor Libros, 2003, page 206.

Panorama (1968), *Cuadernos Hispanoamericanos* (1970), *La Opinión* (1971), *Prensa* (1972), *Noticias* (1973), *Crisis* (1973), *Primera Plana* (1974), *El Auténtico* (1975), and *Informaciones* (1976). Urondo had also won national and international awards for his work in 1966 and 1973. He had augmented his public profile by serving as Director of the Contemporary Art Department at the Universidad Nacional del Litoral (1957), as General Director of Culture in the Ministry of Culture in Santa Fe (1958), and Director of the Department of Literature at the University of Buenos Aires (1973). Most importantly, however, was the fact that he had already been recognized as an active member of the underground guerrilla group, the Revolutionary Armed Forces (*Fuerzas Armadas Revolucionarias*, or *FAR*),[4] and which resulted in his arrest in 1973.

According to the distinguished Rodolfo Walsh,[5] fellow writer and comrade of Urondo in Montoneros, "sending Urondo to Mendoza was a complete mistake." Francisco Urondo was a renowned public figure at that time. Due to his high public profile, leading a life "in hiding, clandestine" in a small city like Mendoza with a close-knit population of 100,000 where "everyone knew each other" was not feasible. Indeed, Francisco Urondo's death was entirely foreseeable. His international fame, which peaked when he was imprisoned in 1973 for his guerrilla connections, practically guaranteed the inevitable failure of the operation. Upon his arrest, a joint committee in support of Urondo was immediately organized

4   FAR was a Marxist and Guevarist organization that merged with Montoneros in 1973.

5   Rodolfo Walsh—second officer and in charge of Press and Intelligence in Montoneros—wrote essential books on the motivation and modus operandi of the military state-terror, such as *Operación masacre* (1957). He also wrote "Carta abierta de un escritor a la Junta Militar," one of the first public letters to denounce the systematic crimes and violations of civil human rights. Rodolfo Walsh paid for his civil disobedience and rebellion with his life: on March 25, 1977, he was kidnapped and disappeared.

in Paris, and hundreds of international intellectuals rallied for his release. A paid advertisement that appeared in mainstream European newspapers was signed by the likes of Marguerite Duras, Jean Paul Sartre, Simone de Beauvoir, Regis Debray, Pier Paolo Pasolini, Gabriel García Márquez, Carlos Fuentes, Jorge Semprún, Julio Cortázar (who published the widely read "Carta muy abierta a Francisco Urondo," or "Very Open Letter to Francisco Urondo," in the newspaper *Libération*), Alberto Moravia, Natalie Sarraute, Paco Ibañez, Malitte Matta, Arturo Jauretche, Juan Gelman, Leónidas Lamborghini, Rodolfo Walsh, David Viñas, Leopoldo Torre Nilson, Leonardo Favio, Leónidas Barletta, and many others.

Despite the foreboding, Urondo faced the challenge with integrity and went to Mendoza immediately, ignoring his father's suggestion to leave the country and turning down his offer of a significant amount of money for that purpose. But once in Mendoza, according to Ernesto Jauretche, Urondo realized that he did not have the support he had been promised:

> In Mendoza, the leaders had fallen. Mendoza was a complex reality and for that reason Paco asked to be updated on what was happening. He needed to know, but nobody knew anything; all he knew was that most of the Montoneros had been captured and taken as prisoners.[6]

Word of Urondo's death came shortly thereafter. On June 17, 1976, following a car chase through the streets of Mendoza, he was assassinated. According to available documents, Urondo was driving a light blue Renault 6. Also in the car were his wife, Alicia Raboy, their baby daughter Ángela, and a fellow Montonero nicknamed "la

---

6 Ernesto Jauretche, cited by Pablo Montanaro in Francisco Urondo. *La palabra en acción. Biografía de un poeta y militante*. Rosario, Santa Fe: Homo Sapiens Ediciones, 2003, page 150.

Turca." They were heading towards the Department of Guaymallén, bordering the city of Mendoza, to meet other Montonero members. The meeting, though, had been "poisoned." In other words, the repressive forces were aware of the arrangements and had prepared an ambush. "La Turca" recounting the tragic events of that afternoon stated:

> We were already on high alert because Varguitas, a *compañero* who lived with us, had been caught, and we had to flee.[7] Another colleague, known as Martín, had disobeyed the order not to return to the house, and one week after Varguitas was caught, the *cana* [police] seized him right there. This Martín, who I know now was actually named Aníbal Torres, was a former police chief from San Juan who had become a *monto* [Montonero]. When he was caught, he betrayed his *compañeros*, and returned to his first love [the police].[8]

Urondo and his passengers quickly noticed the presence of local police personnel, watching and alert, and camouflaged among the neighbors. Shortly thereafter, "la Turca" recognized Martín—the *compañero* who had been arrested—inside a red car that had been taken from the Montoneros in a previous operation. Fearing for his safety and that of his family, Urondo sped along the quiet streets of Guaymallén with the police in pursuit. The chase and gunfire lasted almost 20 minutes. "La Turca" was shot in the leg. Urondo received

---

7 They were told, "Leave the house and go away." Therefore, the sister of Urondo ensures that the vehicle in which they were transported was carrying several suitcases containing their personal effects. They were moving to another house that same afternoon.

8 This text reproduces the declaration of "la Turca." It was recorded by Daniel Desaloms in his documentary *Paco Urondo, la palabra justa*. Buenos Aires: Delta Productions, 2004.

a bullet in the back.

During the confusion, Urondo had been able to get the passengers out of the vehicle. Alicia Raboy ran into a large building supply store and managed to give her baby to an employee of the store before being caught by the police. Her status remains "disappeared" to this day.[9] Their daughter Ángela miraculously survived. "La Turca" escaped by crossing some vacant lots. Urondo who was severely injured remained in the car and continued driving very slowly. Knowing his capture was imminent, he took the cyanide pill[10] he carried in his pocket, a customary practice among the Montoneros when faced with torture and to prevent them from betraying the cause. Before the pill could take effect however, the police captured him alive and forced him to drink gasoline to induce vomiting. They murdered him on the street, shooting him and bashing his head in with a rifle butt. They then stomped out whatever life remained in him.

An eyewitness named Carlos, owner of an auto shop across the street from where Urondo died, confirmed the sequence of events:

> The man (Urondo) had been shot in the back, on the left side. The woman (Alicia Raboy) got out of the vehicle with her baby and started to run, and she threw the baby

---

9 The repression was structured in four stages: kidnapping, torture, imprisonment, and finally, assassination. To avoid legal consequences, there were no official deaths, but rather "disappeared" or "missing" persons. These came to number over 30,000 people, the majority of whom were union members, priests, social activists, human rights lawyers, intellectuals, politicians, and artists like Francisco Urondo. They were all "vanished"—were "disappeared"—during the dark night of this state-sponsored terror imposed by the Argentine dictators.

10 Beatriz Urondo recalls her brother Paco's words: "They will not find me alive, because I love life, but I cannot betray nor harm anyone, so before they get me…." Beatriz Urondo y Germán Amato. *Hermano, Paco Urondo.* Buenos Aires: Nuestra América, 2007.

to one of the men at the building supply store. The other woman (la Turca) started to run and ran past me. She was desperately screaming: 'Where can I escape to? Where can I escape to?' So I guided her through a narrow alley which led into another street; at the end there was a very low adobe wall....

I saw one of those military officers[11] approach the man inside the Renault 6, grab him by the hair, put the revolver to his head and fire. [...] One of the officers said 'all done' and the other replied 'no, it is not done' and threw the man on the ground. When Urondo was on the ground they stepped on his head. After that, another officer came and hit him on his head with the butt of the revolver; but he had already been shot in his head and back.[12]

Francisco Urondo's death came as "...a result of the same series of events that had befallen the majority of those that suffered a similar fate: [...] the chain of fallen *compañeros*, the house [...] searched, the betrayal, and finally, the 'poisoned' meeting."[13]

Urondo's autopsy confirmed the testimony of the witness, Carlos. Two shots, one in the back and one in the head, resulted in "multiple skull fractures, a large hematoma under the chin—in the

---

11 The five police officers allegedly responsible for the death of Urondo and the disappearance of Raboy were later imprisoned for the crimes of kidnapping, torture and murder. Their names and ranks at that time were: Deputy Inspector Juan Agustín Oyarzábal Navarro, Inspector Armando Osvaldo Miranda Fernández, Inspector Eduardo Smaha, First Sergeant of the Federal Police from Mendoza Division Osvaldo Daniel Calegari, and General Commissioner Pedro Dante Sánchez Camargo.

12 Remarks by Carlos, a witness to the murder, according to Rodrigo Sepúlveda in *D2 Documental*, Mendoza, June 18, 2001.

13 Rodolfo Walsh. *Ese hombre y otros papeles*. Buenos Aires: Seix Barral, 1996.

submental artery region—a torn wound in the left ear lobe"[14] and "a star-shaped fracture inflicted by the butt-end of a .45. A pistol-whip."[15]

On his death certificate, Urondo is listed as N.N. (no name). His daughter was transferred to the city's Casa Cuna Number 1 orphanage from where she was then illegally adopted.[16]

There are no official statements regarding the whereabouts of the currently "disappeared" Alicia Raboy. It is known that she was taken to Intelligence Department 2, (D2), one of seven undercover detention centers which existed in Mendoza, and at that time directed by the Chief of Police, vice commodore Santuchone.

The story published in a local newspaper read: "A subversive delinquent was gunned-down in Mendoza. He used a child as a protective shield. They were involved in plans to attack the police station."[17]

with your death
something will come
something that never
disturbed

---

14 Reported by Dr. Raúl Corrandi of Tribunales Forensic Medicine, as collected by Pablo Montanaro, *Francisco Urondo. La Palabra en acción. Biografía de un poeta y militante*. Rosario, Santa Fe: Homo Sapiens, 2003, page 158.

15 Necropsy signed by Dr. De Cicco, according to Pablo Montanaro, *Francisco Urondo. La palabra en acción. Biografía de un poeta y militante*. Rosario, Santa Fe: Homo Sapiens, 2003, page 158.

16 As with hundreds of other stolen babies, it would take Ángela 11 years to "recover her identity" and be able to reunite with her family—her aunt Beatriz and her brother Javier. Hundreds of others are still unaware of their authentic identities. At the time of publication, the human rights group *Abuelas de Plaza de Mayo* has recovered 101 sons and daughters of "disappeared" or "missing" persons.

17 *Los Andes*. Mendoza, June 19, 1976.

your conscience[18]

Urondo's poetry, which up to the moment of his death had continued to evolve as both an art and a means of expression, belonged to the 'innominate' and 'lost' generation of the decades of the 1950s and 1960s. His lyrical work, which showed potential to grow in infinite ways had he not been assassinated, served as a catalyst bringing a fresh new look to the Argentine poetic field during a period of time that was otherwise stagnant.

When the publication of the literary magazine *Martín Fierro* ceased in 1927, there were no significant non-introspective initiatives in the field of poetry. It was not until 1945, with the arrival of Peronism, that new poetic movements and magazines emerged with vigor to revive the lyrical landscape of Argentina.

Among these magazines and literary movements, there were two in which Urondo's participation was noteworthy. The first, the magazine *Poesía Buenos Aires*, was founded in 1950 and became an instigator of one of the most reinvigorating poetic movements of the time. The second, *Zona de la poesía americana*, first published in 1963, made a vast contribution to the much-anticipated new poetic landscape of Argentina. After the founding of these magazines many other publications would follow, bringing new trends to that country.

Apart from the numerous contributions Urondo made to literary magazines and newspapers, he also had a prolific literary output. Urondo's work consisted of strategies and elements that combined the best traditions of Argentine poetry. His early writings: *La Perichole* (1954); *Historia antigua* (1956); *Lugares* (1961); *Dos poemas* (1959) and *Breves* (1959) were highly influenced by surrealism

---

18 Francisco Urondo. "Algo." *Obra poética*. Segunda edición. Buenos Aires: Adriana Hidalgo editora, 2007, page 152.

(hyper-vital) and inventionism (hyper-artistic).[19] The strategies and initiatives he deployed in these pieces also recreated, enhanced and expanded old-style techniques whilst using traditional methods.

It would take Urondo several years to offer a personal vision in a voice of his own, and present an independent poetic identity autonomous from existing movements that abused the introspective and elegiac strategies.

From *Nombres* (1963) to the end of his career, the work of Urondo demonstrated a remarkable twist more consistent with trends linked to the innovative Colloquial Movement so in vogue in the progressive circles of the 1960s. His literary output is best described as poetry associated with the surrounding reality, to the point where in some circles it is referred to as "hyper-social" or "neo-popular" poetry.

This period in his work was marked by its constant commitment to the reality of daily life. In this new stage, Urondo produced some of his best poetry, creating a new way of writing about the turbulent national reality. His voice, with all its colloquial dimensions, was full of choices, renewed colors, and a fresh approach to aspects in terms of literature, but primarily poetry, which previously had been confined to a more narrow perspective. This social colloquialism was clear in all facets of his work. His objective was to motivate his readers. He hoped that by creating a change in the readers it would serve as a catalyst to provoke change in their daily lives.

Urondo created a style which resembled some of the rhetorical methods initiated by the River Plate Region's *Gauchesca* and *Sencillismo* movements which took place in the Nineteenth and Twentieth Centuries, respectively. Urondo found inspiration in a

---

19 César Fernández Moreno distinguished diverse attitudes and currents within the Argentine poetry of that time. Many of them can be found in detail and schematized in his prologue in his book *Antología lineal de la poesía argentina*, published in Madrid, by the publishing house Gredos, in 1968.

variety of schools and Argentine artists of the time, including the simplicity inherent in the verse of Baldomero Fernández Moreno (1886 – 1950) and the Boedo School (*Escuela de Boedo*) of which Raúl Gonzalez Tuñón (1905 – 1974) was the main figure. Also significant were the influences of Oliverio Girondo (1891 – 1967) and of course, Juan Laurentino Ortiz (1896 – 1978), from whom Urondo took his guerrilla war name: "Ortiz."

All these influences and rhetorical strategies were part of an attempt to create a "neo-humanist movement"—a new moral conscience—by melding the direct language of "Conversational Poetry" (*poesía conversacional*) with the imagery of Colloquial Realism (*realismo coloquial*). This new realism also incorporates, to some degree, aspects of the less rhetorically-focused expression of the Antipoetry Movement (*antipoesía*).

Urondo's most significant contribution to the avant-garde movements was to what would later be known as the Socially Conscious Latin American Literature (*literatura comprometida latinoamericana*) and the New Generation of the Sixties (*La Novísima Generación del 60*).

The philosophy of his work, greatly revered amongst these movements, may be associated alongside the works of writers such as Nicanor Parra (Chile 1914), Ernesto Cardenal (Nicaragua 1925), Javier Heraud (Peru 1942 – 1963), Enrique Lihn (Chile 1929 – 1988), Antonio Cisneros (Peru 1942), Roberto Fernández Retamar (Cuba 1930), Jorge Enrique Adoum (Ecuador 1926 – 2009), and Roque Dalton (El Salvador 1935 – 1975).

Julia Leverone's *Fuel and Fire* is excellent news for those who love the poetry of Paco Urondo and for those researchers who are revisiting and revising the critical understanding of Argentine history during the military *junta*. Urondo did not believe in borders, neither geographical nor linguistic, as his suffering and his thinking were internationalist. The translation into English of his poetry, which Urondo would surely have found moving, begins a new journey, which hopefully can excite and subvert biased historiographies. This book will be a rich source of information for scholars who explore the always dramatic relationship among dictatorship, social politics, and poetry.

Francisco Urondo

Fuel and Fire

Selected Poems 1956–1976
Translated by Julia Leverone

a Ángela y Javier
a Alicia y Claudia

a Edgar y Noé

Ojos grandes, serenos

Andando, el barro nos llega a las caderas. Calmando algunas
inquietudes, han nacido otras. Rodamos sobre nuevos
remansos.

Nadie vuelve; es ahora el momento del amor. El deseo es una
ola suave; aquí en la orilla, con la mano firme, detrás de los
juncos, frente al sol.

Volarán los pájaros silvestres, las islas vencerán a las palabras: el
silencio sagrado sobre el mundo.

Iremos a la hoguera con los grandes herejes.

Large, Calm Eyes

Going forth, the mud comes up to our hips. Calming some
  uncertainties, giving rise to others. We rove around new
  pools.

No one returns; now is the moment for love. Desire is a soft
  wave; here on the shore, with a firm hand, behind the dried
  reeds, before the sun.

The wild birds will take flight, the islands will overcome words:
  sacred silence over the earth.

We will go toward the fire together with the great heretics.

Cuerpo del delito

Los balcones de Aranjuez, las sedas
que caen sobre el río verde; me desperezo
como una columna y penetro tus enaguas, abanico
tu tristeza palaciega, tu cuerda
de laúd hechizado por los temblores de tu cuerpo, me
voy de madre
a padre y a lecho nuevamente, sintiendo cómo
los hombros suben hasta mi pecho y
te transfiguro en una gran espalda que voy
lamiendo de rodillas. No hablemos
de aquellos vahos, podemos
enjuagar el paladar de uno en el paladar
del otro, con las aguas verdes
que desbordan sobre tus ojos encendidos
ahora de tanto volar, de tantos
caminos; un poco de calor. Una mano
quedó en alto saludando tus pañuelos, tu aliento
ebrio de Aranjuez, de este olor que te soplo
desde tan lejos, con tanta
fuerza para que lo recibas en tu Puerto
y le permitas cargar la carne
salada, el agua potable, los vientos de la partida, los
cabos para ceñir los desengaños, para
trincar la suerte sobre el cuerpo del muelle.

Toda la serenidad para ver la cara
abrevada, de virgen-hombre, harta

Body of Crime

The balconies of Aranjuez, the silks
that fall on the green river: I stretch myself
like a column and penetrate your underskirts, fan
your palatial sadness, your pendant's
chain bewitched by the tremors of your body, I
go from mother
to father to the bed again, feeling how
your shoulders rise up to my chest and
I transfigure you into one whole great back I go on
to lick, on my knees. Let's not speak
of those breaths, we can
rinse one palate with the palate
of the other, with the green waters
that spill from your eyes burning
now from so much flight, so many
paths; a bit of heat. A hand
remained high waving your handkerchiefs, your breath
drunken with the Aranjuez, with this scent that I blow to you
from so far, with enough force
so that you can receive in your port
and allow the loading of the salted
meat, the potable water, the winds of departure, the
ropes to stay the disillusions, to
tie luck to the body of the dock.

All the serenity to see the watered
face, that of the man-virgin, fed up

de astucias, de mi amigo Julio Lareu.

Su cara flanqueada por dos hijitas,
humilde y el colmo
de la bondad de mi amigo Julio Lareu.

Hombre de catadura, queriendo
a sus criaturas, corazón alzado
en los rastros de mi amigo Julio Lareu.

Vengo a desear nada más
que tu buenaventura
amigo, carpintero.

with all the ruses, of my friend Julio Lareu.

His face flanked by two small daughters,
humble and the height
of the goodness of my friend Julio Lareu.

A man of values, loving
his children, heart resurrected
in the traces of my friend Julio Lareu.

I come to desire nothing more
than your good fortune
friend, carpenter.

La pura verdad

Si ustedes lo permiten,
prefiero seguir viviendo.

Después de todo y de pensarlo bien, no tengo
motivos para quejarme o protestar:

siempre he vivido en la gloria: nada
importante me ha faltado.

Es cierto que nunca quise imposibles; enamorado
de las cosas de este mundo con inconsciencia y dolor y miedo y
    apremio.

Muy de cerca he conocido la imperdonable alegría; tuve sueños
    espantosos y buenos amores, ligeros y culpables.

Me avergüenza verme cubierto de pretensiones; una gallina
    torpe,
melancólica, débil, poco interesante,

un abanico de plumas que el viento desprecia,
caminito que el tiempo ha borrado.

Los impulsos mordieron mi juventud y ahora, sin darme cuenta,
    voy iniciando
una madurez equilibrada, capaz de enloquecer a cualquiera o
    aburrir de golpe.

The Plain Truth

If you, sirs, would permit it,
I'd prefer to go on living.

After everything and having thought it over carefully, I have
no motives to protest or complain:

I have always lived in glory: I have never
lacked anything necessary.

It's correct that I never wanted the impossible; enamored
of the things of this world unconsciously and with pain and
    fear and urgency.

Very closely, I have known unforgivable happiness; I have had
startling dreams and good romances, swift and implicating.

It's shameful seeing myself covered in pretenses; a clumsy
    chicken,
melancholy, weak, of little interest,

a fan of feathers the wind dispels,
a footpath time has scratched.

Impulses bit into my youth and now, without realizing it, I'm
    entering
into a balanced maturity, capable of driving anyone insane or
    boring them quickly.

Mis errores han sido olvidados definitivamente; mi memoria ha
    muerto y se queja
con otros dioses varados en el sueño y los malos sentimientos.

El perecedero, el sucio, el futuro, supo acobardarme, pero lo he
    derrotado para siempre; sé que futuro y memoria se vengarán
    algún día.

Pasaré desapercibido, con falsa humildad, como la Cenicienta,
    aunque algunos
me recuerden con cariño o descubran mi zapatito y también
    vayan muriendo.

No descarto la posibilidad
de la fama y del dinero; las bajas pasiones y la inclemencia.

La crueldad no me asusta y siempre viví
deslumbrado por el puro alcohol, el libro bien escrito, la carne
    perfecta.

Suelo confiar en mis fuerzas y en mi salud
y en mi destino y en la buena suerte:

sé que llegaré a ver la revolución, el salto temido
y acariciado, golpeando a la puerta de nuestra desidia.

Estoy seguro de llegar a vivir en el corazón de una palabra;
compartir este calor, esta fatalidad que quieta no sirve y se
    corrompe.

My mistakes have been entirely forgotten; my memory has died
    and it complains
with the other gods stranded in sleep and in doubt.

The perishable, the dirty, the future knew to daunt me, but I
    have defeated them
forever; I know that future and memory will prevail one day.

I will pass unnoticed, with false humility, like Cinderella,
    although some
might remember me with affection or discover my little shoe
    and also go on to die.

I won't discard the possibility
of fame and money; carnal passions and inclemency.

Cruelty doesn't frighten me and I always lived
floored by good alcohol, a well-written book, perfectly-done
    meat.

I tend to trust my strength and my health
and my destiny and good luck:

I know that I will come to see the revolution, that feared
and cherished leap, banging on the door of our apathy.

I am sure of coming to live in the heart of a word;
sharing this heat, this fatality that, quieted, becomes worthless
    and rots.

Puedo hablar y escuchar la luz
y el color de la piel amada y enemiga y cercana.

Tocar el sueño y la impureza,
nacer con cada temblor gastado en la huida.

Tropiezos heridos de muerte;
esperanza y dolor y cansancio y ganas.

Estar hablando, sostener
esta victoria, este puño; saludar, despedirme.

Sin jactancias puedo decir
que la vida es lo mejor que conozco.

I can speak and listen to the light
and color of the skin of a lover and an enemy and a close friend.

Touch dream and defect,
be born with each tremble of escape.

Stumblings, fatal wounds;
hope and pain and weariness and will.

To be speaking, to hold
this victory, this fist; to wave hello, goodbye.

Without disdain I can say
that life is the best that I know.

Escola do samba

Me aburro dando vueltas;
más que bailar prefiero quedarme sentado
escuchando la música.

Es difícil perder el tiempo
o ganarlo. Es difícil ser torpe. Tener ocasiones en la vida.
Hay que actuar con naturalidad, ser espontáneo, estar
muy loco o muy decidido.

El cuerpo de mi compañera de baile cruje bajo mi brazo. Ese
mismo cuerpo fue apretado por amor y no importa;
deslumbrado por fantasías incuestionables;
por esta nueva forma de impaciencia.

Era la voz de Fiorentino, la voz ausente y suntuosa
   del caído
que hubiese necesitado escuchar con toda violencia.

No sabemos escuchar;
nos gusta ir haciendo cualquier cosa para destruirnos,
olvidar un tango cantado de esa manera tan perfecta.

Nadie quiere sentir ningún rojo sonido,
nadie quiere escuchar ese cuerpo encendido que conozco
nadie sabe y todos quieren bailar aunque no sepan,
aunque caigan sin destreza, sin tiempo.

Escola do Samba

I get bored turning in circles;
more than dancing I'd rather stay sitting,
listening to the music.

It's difficult to lose the rhythm
or to find it. It's difficult to be clumsy. To have chances in life.
You have to behave naturally, be spontaneous, be
very erratic or very decided.

My dance partner's body crosses under my arm. That
same body was burdened by love and it doesn't matter;
dazzled by unquestionable fantasies;
by this new form of impatience.

It was the voice of Fiorentino, the absent and sumptuous voice
   of the fallen
that she would have needed to hear with full violence.

We don't know how to listen;
we like to go on doing whatever thing to ruin ourselves,
to forget a tango sung in that perfect way.

No one wants to hear a single red sound,
no one wants to listen to that ignited body that I know,
no one knows and everyone wants to dance even if they don't know,
even if they fall without distress, without rhythm.

Y bailamos toda la noche atrapados por esa música de barrio,
toda la noche bailamos ese tango confuso;

seducidos durante todo el mundo,
dando vueltas como animales perdidos.

And we dance the whole night trapped by that barrio music,
all night we dance that confused tango;

seduced meanwhile the whole world,
turning in circles like lost animals.

Leña y fuego

a Luis Yadarola

Tus labios palpitan en la roja y fluctuante llama. Tus labios y esa
dura leña que gira en el espacio. Todo es manso y soberbio: el
terso amanecer, el suave seno.

Alguien se salva masticando su culpa y tirando las ilusiones a
los perros.

Tus labios se mueven; bailan al ritmo de las caprichosas idas y
venidas del fuego del mundo.

Amo el viento y el ardor del verano.

Fuel and Fire

For Luis Yadarola

Your lips pulse in the red and fluctuating flame. Your lips and
that hard firewood that turns in the space. Everything is quiet
and magnificent: the smooth dawn, your soft breast.

Someone saves themselves by chewing their guilt and throwing
illusions to the dogs.

Your lips move; they dance to the rhythm of the capricious
comings and goings of the fire of the world.

I love the wind and the burning of summer.

No puedo quejarme

Estoy con pocos amigos y los que hay
suelen estar lejos y me ha quedado
un regusto que tengo al alcance de la mano
como un arma de fuego. La usaré para nobles
empresas: derrotar al enemigo —salud
y suerte—, hablar humildemente
de estas posibilidades amenazantes.

Espero que el rencor no intercepte
el perdón, el aire
lejano de los afectos que preciso: que el rigor
no se convierta en el vidrio de los muertos; tengo
curiosidad por saber qué cosas dirán de mí; después
de mi muerte; cuáles serán tus versiones del amor, de estas
afinidades tan desencontradas,
porque mis amigos suelen ser como las señales
de mi vida, una suerte trágica, dándome
todo lo que no está. Prematuramente, con un pie
en cada labio de esta grieta que se abre
a los pies de mi gloria: saludo a todos, me tapo
la nariz y me dejo tragar por el abismo.

I Cannot Complain

I have few friends left and those who are here
are usually far and I am left
an aftertaste I hold within reach
as if a firearm. I'll use it for noble
reasons: for defeating the enemy—salud
y suerte—, for speaking modestly
about these threatening possibilities.

I hope bitterness won't intercept
forgiveness, that distant
air of affect I'm describing: that the rigor
won't convert into the glass of the dead; I am
curious to know the things they'll say about me; after
my death; which were your versions of love, of these
similarities so separated,
because my friends tend to be like the signals
of my life, a tragic luck, giving me
all that isn't here. Prematurely, with a foot
on each lip of this crevice that opens
at the feet of my glory: I salute you all, I hold
my nose, and let the abyss surround me.

Milonga del marginado paranóico

Parece mentira
que haya llegado a tener
la culpa de todo lo que ocurre
en el mundo: pero es así. Han tratado
de disuadirme psicólogos y sociólogos de mi tiempo,
me han dado razones de peso técnico largamente
formuladas y
parcialmente ciertas. Pero
yo sé que soy culpable de los dolores
que aquí siento y recorren el mundo; de las soledades
que lo van vaciando: quisiera saltar
como Juan L. Ortiz, vociferar
como Oliverio Girondo, pero: primero, ellos me ganaron
de mano; segundo, no me sale bien y aquí
empieza todo nuevamente: otro sufrimiento
igual a diapasones y recursos
que conozco perfectamente y que no vale la pena
repetir: primero, para no emularlos; segundo, porque tendré que
    ir
reconociendo que no he sabido
hacerme entender. Y esto es agudo como un ataque
que nos traga la lengua; pido entonces disculpas
por la mala impresión, por las exageraciones.

Milonga of the Marginalized Paranoid

It seems a lie
that I've come to be
at fault for everything that happens
in the world: but it's true. They've tried
to dissuade me, psychologists and sociologists of my time,
they've given reasons of a technical weight long
in form and
partially right. But
I know I'm guilty of the pain
I feel here and rampant in the world; of the solitude
that empties it further: I would've liked to leap
like Juan L. Ortiz, speak out
like Oliverio Girondo, but: first, they got
the upper hand; second, neither action really suits me and here
everything begins again. Another suffering
equal to tuning forks and options
I'm well aware of that aren't worth
repeating: first, to not emulate them; second, because I'll have
    to go on
recognizing that I haven't known
how to make myself understand. And that's as sharp
as an attack that swallows our tongues; I ask then for you to excuse
the bad impression, the exaggerations.

Benefacción

Piedad para los equivocados, para
los que apuraron el paso y los torpes
de lentitud. Para los que hablaron bajo tortura
o presión de cualquier tipo, para los que supieron
callar a tiempo o no pudieron mover
un dedo; perdón por los desaires con que me trata
la suerte; por titubeos y balbuceos. Perdón
por el campo que crece en estos espacios de la época
trabajosa, soberbia. Perdón
por dejarse acunar entre huesos
y tierras, sabihondos y suicidas, ardores
y ocasos, imaginaciones perdidas y penumbras.

Kindness

Give mercy to the mistaken, to
those who quickened their step and those
clumsily slow. To those who spoke under torture
or whatever kind of pressure, to those who knew
to quiet in time or couldn't move
a finger; forgiveness for the disdain with which luck
has treated me; for hesitations and mutterings. Forgiveness
for the countryside that grows in these spaces of an era
arduous, arrogant. Forgiveness
for allowing to swing between bones
and lands, smart-asses and suicidals, burning
and twilight, imaginations lost and half-lit.

Hoy un juramento

Cuando esta casa,
en la que vivo hace años,
tenga
una salida, yo cerraré
la puerta para guardar su calor;

yo la abriré
para que los vientos
de todas partes, vengan
a lavarle la cara;

a remontarla,
de esa manera con que vuelan
las intenciones,
los aparecidos, los recuerdos por venir,
y lo que a uno le asusta
aunque todavía no haya ocurrido.

Today, a Hearing

When this house,
in which I have lived for years,
has
an exit, I'll close
the door to keep its heat;

I'll open it
so the winds
from all parts will come
to clean its face;

to lift it
in that way in which intentions
fly,
apparitions, memories to come,
and what startles you
though it hasn't yet occurred.

Mosquitos

Extiende la mano y espanta esos mosquitos.

Favoréceme: son insectos hambrientos, es la primera mujer que
hemos tenido y apenas reconocemos ahora; son los años que
hemos olvidado en algún tren: sólo les queda la amenaza, el
sopor y una simple esperanza.

Carga sobre mi espalda lo que has abolido de mi pecho.

Mosquitoes

Reach out your hand and swat those mosquitoes.

Hear me out; they're hungry insects, she's the first woman
we've ever had and scarcely recognize, now; those are the
years we've forgotten on some train: all that's left for them is
threat, drowsiness, and a simple hope.

Load on my back what you've carved from my chest.

Felipe Vallese

Escuché que unos chicos preguntaron: "quién parará la lluvia"; otras
personas estaban escuchando la misma pregunta y, a su vez, comenzaron
a formularla: el dependiente, el despachante de bebidas
de importación; hasta pulperos y uruguayitas y otros
hermanos continentales abandonaban la vieja y estúpida
rivalidad, despejando las nubes de misterio
y confusión sobre la tierra, para preguntar precisamente: "who'll
stop the rain". Guardianes del orden se aventuraron
en la desesperación para preguntarse también: "quién parará
la lluvia" y la pregunta rodó de mano en mano, hasta llegar a los oídos
acolchonados de torturadores, especialistas de toda calaña que nunca
pudieron zambullirse en la gloria del sol: "Quién parará la lluvia", decían
unos y otros y los tontos y los pillos trataban de conjurar
el clamor, los nuevos aires que se desataban con las lluvias, el amor
que arranca con las tormentas: "quién parará la lluvia", decían los enfermos,
los desamparados, los derrotados y los satisfechos que dejaron de serlo
inmediatamente después de preguntar "quién parará la lluvia". De inmediato
los éxitos se derrumbaron como pestes triunfales, el New Deal se enredó
en sus cadenas doradas, el doctor Frondizi no se dio cuenta. Los muertos
se plegaron al desafío: asesinados llegaron
a levantar la cabeza lacerada y miraron de frente,
requiriendo; "quién parará la lluvia". Y la pregunta se generalizó
como los temporales, empujó
los cielos y abrió las luces del espacio.

Felipe Vallese

I heard that some boys asked: "who'll stop the rain"; other
people heard the same question and, in turn, began
to form it: the store clerk, the customs
officer; even pulperos and uruguayitas and other
continental brothers abandoned their old and stupid
rivalry, clearing the clouds of mystery
and confusion over the earth, to ask precisely: *who'll*
stop the rain. Keepers of the order adventured
in their desperation to ask themselves as well: "who'll stop
the rain" and the question rolled from hand to hand, until it came
to the cushioned ears of torturers, specialists of all kinds who never
could plunge into the glory of the sun: "Who'll stop the rain," they said
one and all and the stupid and the petty thieves tried to capture
the clamor, the new airs that loosed with the rains, the love
that uproots with the storms: "who'll stop the rain," said the sick,
the defenseless, the defeated, and the satisfied who stopped being so
immediately after asking "who'll stop the rain." All of a sudden
victories collapsed like triumphant plagues, the New Deal tangled
in its golden chains, Doctor Frondizi didn't notice. The dead
yielded to the defiance; the assassinated came
to raise their lacerated heads and gaze ahead,
demanding: "who'll stop the rain." And the question spread
like the seasonal storms, shoved against
the sky, and opened to the lights of the universe.

Por soledades

Un hombre es perseguido, una
familia entera, una organización, un pueblo. La
responsable de esta situación no es la codicia, sino un
comerciante con sus precios, con la imposición
de las reglas del juego. Los empresarios, la policía
con la imposición de las reglas del juego. Por eso
ese hombre, ese pueblo, esa familia, esa organización, se
siente perseguida. Es más, comienzan
a perseguirse entre ellos, a delatarse,
a difamarse, y juntos, a su vez, se lanzan a perseguir
quimeras, a olvidarse de las legítimas,
de las costosas pero realizables aspiraciones;
marginan la penosa esperanza. Entonces
toda la familia, todo el pueblo, entra
en el nivel más alto de la persecución: la paranoia, esa
refinada búsqueda de los
perseguidos históricos y culturales.
Y ésta
es la triste historia de los pueblos
derrotados, de las familias envilecidas,
de las organizaciones inútiles, de los hombres solitarios, la
llama que se consume sin el viento, los aires
que soplan sin amor, los amores que se marchitan
sobre la memoria del amor o sus fatuas presunciones.

For Solitudes

One man is persecuted, an
entire family, an organization, a people. The
entity responsible in this situation is not greed, but
a businessman with a price, with an imposition
of the rules of the game. The entrepreneurs, the police,
with an imposition of the rules of the game. That's why
that man, that people, that family, that organization
feel persecuted. What's more, they begin
to accuse one another, to betray one another,
to slander one another, and together, in turn, launch pursuits
of chimeras, forget the legitimate,
the costly but attainable dreams;
they reduce pitiful hope. So
the whole family, the whole people, enter
into the highest level of persecution: paranoia, that
fastidious search of the
historically and culturally persecuted.
And this
is the sad story of a defeated
people, of degraded families,
of useless organizations, of lonely men, the
flame that consumes itself without wind, the airs
that blow without love, the love that withers
on the memory of love or its fatuous presumptions.

Carlos Gardel

Extranjero del silencio
en el mundo arrasado; vertiente de la extrema melancholia
y del coraje y de la velocidad del amor y del miedo.

Dueño de la ciudad, de su memoria blanda
y de la madrugada hambrienta y sin sentimientos
y de la suprema cordura de los vagos.

Cómplice de los encuentros,
de la grappa que nos hizo hablar,
loco de la noche, despreocupado amigo del alba, *señor
de los tristes.*

Carlos Gardel

Stranger to silence
in the razed world; gradient of extreme melancholy
and courage and the velocity of love and fear.

Owner of this city, of its soft memory
and of the starved, numbed dawn
and of the supreme cognizance of vagabonds.

Accomplice of encounters
and of the grappa that made us speak,
lunatic of the night, unconcerned friend of the dawn, *leader*
of the forlorn.

Liliana Raquel Gelin

Como un viejo guerrero, tirando
un manojo de luz a la cara
de los sombríos, ha muerto
una chica de veinte años; pudo
ser mi hija. Avilantez
sobrevolaban su vuelo, amarraron
su aire; no es la muchacha
colgada del frágil designio.

Aquí habrá batalla como en los campos
de Córdoba, rayo de dolor, escalofrío
donde murió valientemente una chica
de veinte años: hijita mía,
palomita tremenda, duérmase
mi niña, duérmase mi son que ya nadie
la va a molestar. El Cuco será derrotado
y sus hermanitos y padres cuidarán
de su jardín, regirán los reflejos de su pasado.

Que haya paz en su memoria
por la que vive. Que haya eterna
gratitud por su generosidad eterna.

Liliana Raquel Gelin

Like an old war hero, casting
a torch in the face
of the dismal, a girl
of twenty years has died; she could
have been my daughter. Insolent
they flew over her flight, they tied off
her air; the young woman not
hung from a fragile plan.

Here there will be battle as in the fields
of Córdoba, a bolt of pain, a shiver
where valiantly a girl
of twenty died: my little darling,
tremendous dove, sleep
my child, sleep my sound for no one
will bother you again. Cuco will be defeated
and her brothers and fathers will care
for her garden, will rule over the light of her past.

Let there be peace in her memory
for she who lives. Let there be eternal
gratitude for her eternal generosity.

Amarla es difícil

Es buena, cuando duerme;
el calor de su cuerpo es un puñal de vidrio
que remonta los sueños.

Cuando calla, es buena
y su voz una premonición olvidada y peligrosa
que arruina el silencio.

Cuando grita o llora
o se lamenta o se divierte o se cansa,
nada puede contener
este dolor alegre que envenena
mis sueños y mi soledad.
Por eso es difícil pensar
en ella, en su cara bondadosa;
abandonarse; por eso
es una cobardía retenerla
y dejarla ir, una pavorosa crueldad.
A veces, cuando lo pienso,
no sé qué hacer con ella,
con este destino luminoso.

Loving Her Is Difficult

She's good, when she sleeps;
the heat of her body is a dagger of glass
that gains on dreams.

When she quiets, she's good,
and her voice a forgotten and perilous premonition
that wrecks silence.

When she shouts or cries
or laments or plays or tires
nothing can contain
this lively pain that poisons
my dreams and my solitude.
That's why it's difficult to think
of her, of her kind face;
to give over; that's why
it's cowardice to keep her
and to let her go, a horrific cruelty.
Sometimes, considering it,
I don't know what to do with her,
with this luminous destiny.

Dame la mano

Cuando arda el amor,
no estaré a tu lado,
estaré lejos.

Será por cobardía,
por no sufrir,
por no reconocer que no supe
cambiar todo esto.

Arderá el amor,
arderá su memoria
hasta que todo sea como lo soñamos
como en realidad pudo haber sido.

Pero ya estaré lejos.
Será tarde para lamentos
y nadie podrá todavía asombrarse
de lo que tiene.

Antes que nada, antes
de sospechar,
vivamos esto, que más no sea, y que
por ahí es demasiado.

Vivir, sin
que nadie admita; abrir el fuego
hasta que el amor, rezongando, arda
como si entrara en el porvenir.

Give Me Your Hand

When love burns,
I won't be beside you,
I'll be far.

It'll be out of cowardice,
for not suffering,
for not acknowledging that I didn't know
how to change all this.

Love will burn,
its memory will burn
until all is as we dreamed
which in reality it could have been.

But I'll be far already.
It'll be late for regret
and no one will still be able to be surprised
by what they've got.

Before all else, before
suspicion,
let's live this, which may not be much, and which
over there may be excessive.

To live, with
no one admitting it; to open the fire
until love, groaning, burns
as if it entered the future.

Días estos y aquellos

Ha oído el sol de invierno. Crece envolviendo y ajustando su
corazón; sacude su sueño, despliega las plumas que le abrigan:
ve caer aquí o allá el contorno de sus ídolos.

El calor no lo matará del todo; el frío no quebrantará su
sueño. Herido está de tiempo que lo contiene, de crueldad,
de decisión, de grandes dársenas, de eterno comienzo, de
mesurado adiós.

Days Come and Gone

The winter sun has heard. It grows casting layers around and
adjusting its heart; it shakes off sleep, unfurls the feather coat
it wears: looks on as the shapes of its idols fall here and there.

Heat won't kill it fully, cold won't burst its sleep. It's wounded
by time that contains it, by cruelty, by decision, by great
docks, by eternal beginning, by measured goodbyes.

Algo

a Rubén Rodríguez Aragón

con tu muerte
algo vendrá
algo que jamás sacudió
tu conciencia

no importará
la tierra que te rodea
el árbol que te soporta
el agua que admitió tu pereza

no será algo
que ahora retumba en tu memoria
ni las resonancias que prefirió olvidar

vendrá algo sin vínculos
una lluvia sin pasado
sin gestos censurables
o bondadosos

no estará en juego
tu salvación
tampoco el olvido
ni el arrepentimiento

el «ángel tuerto»

Something

For Rubén Rodríguez Aragón

when you die
something will come
something never shaken off
by your conscience

it won't matter
the earth that surrounds you
the tree underneath you
the water that admitted your laziness

it won't be something
that now resounds in your memory
nor the resonances it preferred to forget

something will come without ties
an ahistorical rain
no censurable
or generous gestures

your salvation
or oblivion
or remorse
won't be in play

the "one-eyed angel"

no vendrá a consolarte
no será necesario
y olvidarás también el consuelo

para tu corazón
no habrá consuelo el día en que caigas

no habrá estaciones
ni pájaros
ni trenes
ni alcohol
ni sangre penosa que aguantar

no por eso habrá descanso
el día en que llegue algo que no suponías
algo que vendrá a reclamar
el lugar en el mundo
que supiste negarle

una indescriptible culpa
haciendo estallar las huellas
que minuciosamente lograbas distribuir

ningún rastro

con tu muerte
vendrá una nueva
y desconocida vergüenza

won't come to console you
it won't be necessary
and you'll forget the comfort too

for your heart
there will be no consolation the day that you fall

there won't be seasons
or birds
or trains
or alcohol
or terrible blood to endure

there won't be rest that follows
the day when something arrives you didn't suspect
when something will come to reclaim
the place in the world
you knew to deny it

an indescribable guilt
exploding the traces
you meticulously managed to leave

traceless

with your death
will come a new
and unknown shame

Vampiresa

Oh Isabel de Baviera, por qué esconderse tanto, ninfómana
de cabecera de alguien: siempre desconcertando
agitando hechos previsibles, pero inesperados: dabas
a entender otra cosa.

Siempre siendo otra, escurriendo realidades inoportunas
de tan ocultas; otra, con una voluntad de monarca. Qué lástima
que hayas andado hiriendo de semejante manera, Isabel
de Baviera; escapando a la gente y a sus nobles objetos; un
exorcismo innecesario, impúdico, parpadeando
en estos y otros ojos que también me pertenecen.

Sorteando obstáculos, has sido
otra para ver otros
en los otros: cuánto cansancio del cansancio, aunque
haya habido éxitos, producido milagros, porque a veces
los otros verdaderamente fueron otros y después se han
pasado la vida echando esos extraños de su casa.

No sabría encontrar ahora tus facciones, cómo
describirlas: todas escapan de su lugar y ocupan
otros lugares, como los malos espíritus, otras personas
buscándose un rincón en el tiempo, un cuerpo, una
historia personal que corre a esconderse en las cuevas
de Transilvania, Isabel de Baviera: Ah, si te hubieras
   conformado
con vivir en tus tierras, sin ganar mundos, sin dañar a la gente.

Vampiress

Oh Isabel of Bavaria, why hide yourself so much, nymphomaniac
at somebody's headboard: always disconcerting
causing incidents predictable, but unexpected: you made
something else known.

Always being another, draining unfortunate realities
so secretly; another, with a monarch's drive. A shame
you've not stopped wounding in such a way, Isabel
of Bavaria; escaping the people and their noble objectives; an
unnecessary exorcism, immodest, blinking
into these and other eyes that are also mine.

Dodging obstacles, you have been
another for seeing others
in the others: how much exhaustion of exhaustion, though
there have been successes, miracles made, because sometimes
the others really were others and afterward have
gone through life casting those strangers from their homes.

Now I wouldn't know how to recognize your features, how
to describe them: they all escape from their place and occupy
other places, like bad spirits, other people
looking for their corner in time, a body, a
personal history that runs for cover in the caves
of Transylvania, Isabel of Bavaria: Ah, if you had only resigned
to living in your lands, without wanting worlds, without
　　hurting the people.

Adioses

A cierta edad, los allegados se alejan, empiezan
a morir. Murió Oliverio y todo el continente
también murió entre los cóndores diez meses después para poder
erguir sus cerbatanas; murieron lugartenientes, gladiadores
anónimos. Se ha muerto últimamente
de mala manera y así se seguirá muriendo, como
estaba previsto: Emilio (al que le toque) de espaldas en el suelo,
tratando de sacar, o no sacar el arma; murió el petiso
aquel, corrector del diario, también entre las grandes
aves de rapiña. Murió mi eternidad,
pero nadie se ha dispuesto a velarla; a lo mejor
muere Beatriz con quien jugamos siempre
como si fuéramos criaturas predestinadas, secretamente,
para no romper el sortilegio y perder blasones y ganar
realidades. Murió el bravo capoerista frente a la obra
en construcción, entre un agitar de sotanas
enfiladas sobre rumbos inciertos. En fin, murieron
algunas personas de mi amistad; otras que conozco
de vista seguramente han muerto. Celia murió, pero
hace muchos años, aunque a veces sueño con ella desnuda
y viva como los arcángeles con toda su música. Murió Moisés
Lebensohn y no podía ocurrir otra cosa
con ciertas ideas: hubo muchos infartos
y cirrosis −oh gran rey− en la boca
de mis pulmones que recuerdan
a presión que olvidan
a sabiendas. Mis hijos viven, pero ya ni se acuerdan

Goodbyes

At a certain age, those close to you become distant, begin
to die. Oliverio died and the whole continent
also died among the condors ten months later to be able
to raise its blowguns; landholders died, anonymous
gladiators. Those who have died lately
have done so poorly and so they will continue to die, as
was foretold: Emilio (whose turn it is) on his back on the floor,
trying or not trying to take out his gun; that short guy
died, the newspaper editor, also among the great
raptors. My eternity has died,
but no one's come out to mourn it. Beatriz
may die with whom we always played
as if we were children predestined, in secret,
to not break the spell and lose blazons and gain
realities. The brave capoerista died before the work
under construction, among a rustling of robes
strung on uncertain tracks. In sum,
people who were my friends died; others I recognize
have surely also died. Celia died, but
years ago, though sometimes I dream of her naked
and alive like the archangels with all their music. Moisés
Lebensohn died and no other thing could have happened
with certain ideas: there were many heart attacks
and cirrhosis—oh great king—in the mouth
of my lungs that remember
under pressure that they forget
in full knowledge. My children live, but don't remember anymore

de quién era la tía Teodolinda
que también murió. Compañeros del colegio han muerto, apósteles
y simples camaradas de armas y deportes. Hasta enemigos
y también hombres, a quienes me ligaban simpatías enfermas −me
refiero a algunos comerciantes fallecidos−, pero justas, inevitables
como la muerte. Puedo estar contento
de estar vivo: abro los ojos, salto
de la cama, me visto, salgo a esperar otros años, como ahora
que cierro la puerta, miro hacia atrás la primera mitad
del camino y busco los lugares para emboscarme
a cara descubierta, a golpes. Alegrías pesarosas, funerales.

Del excusado al lavatorio salta
mi corazón como si fuera
un jabón. Puedo tener el mundo
en mis manos, dijo Beethoven y también
lo podría decir yo, si no fuera
por este jabón que se resbala
de las manos y nadie
lo quiere por eso, a pesar
de que haya lavado más de una cara,
arrastrado alguna mugre, hojas
en el otoño; subestiman
su espuma dejándolo gastar
de aquí para allá, del excusado
al lavatorio, diluido
en el agua caliente que ahogará
las risas de los arrepentidos.

who their Aunt Teodolinda was
who also died. Classmates have died, apostles,
and simple comrades in arms and sports. Even enemies
and men who I was linked to by sick sympathy—I'm referring
to a few fallen businessmen—, but fair, inevitable
as death. I can be content
to be living: I open my eyes, jump
from bed, dress, leave to wait for other years, like now
that I've closed the door, I see behind me the first half
of the way and look for places to lie in ambush
barefaced, beneath blows. Saddened contentment, funereal.

From the one excused to the bathroom leaps
my heart as if it were a piece
of soap. I can take the world
into my hands, said Beethoven, and I
could say it too, if it weren't
for this soap that slips
from my grasp and so
nobody wants it, despite
the fact it's washed more than one face,
drawn some grime, leaves
in autumn; they underestimate
its suds letting it expend
from here to there, from the one excused
to the bathroom, diluted
in the hot water that will drown
the laughter of the repentant.

Tinieblas para mirar

Veo tus intenciones y tus actos
triunfales por crecer; adivino el parpadeo, veo
y quisiera descansar
un poco, se entiende. Veo los tiempos
ocultos, las intenciones
de mal y viceversa. Veo palabras que no fueron
articuladas, escenarios, disfraces vulgares, caracterizaciones. Veo
jactancias, humildades
apócrifas y bastante
sufrimiento disimulado. Veo la luz
compartida de las inconsciencias, veo,
veo, una ramita, de qué color: no puedo decirlo. El
tamaño, la disposición, las significaciones, las alegrías
se disuelven, se resbalan en los aceites que hierven
y respiramos sin tocar, para no ir quemando estos ardidos
corazones, este impromptus venéreo como
las mejillas, como las ramas de qué colores
insignificantes, de qué adioses
aterrados, más que de frío, por los calores iniciales del miedo.

Shadows for Seeing

I see your intentions and triumphal
acts still to grow; I can intuit a blink, I see
and would like to rest a little,
understandably. I see dark
times, bad
intentions and vice versa. I see words that weren't
spoken, scenarios, vulgar costumes, characterizations. I see
boastfulness, apocryphal
humility and much
hidden suffering. I see the light
shared by unconsciousnesses, I see,
I see, a small branch, what color: I can't say. The
size, the position, the significances, the happinesses
dissolve, slip into the boiling acids
and we breathe without touching, to not go on burning these fiery
hearts, this spontaneity venereal like
cheeks, like the branches of which insignificant
colors, of which goodbyes
petrified, more than by cold, by the initial heats of fear.

Otra cosa

Queridos hijitos, su papá poco sabe de ustedes
y sufre por esto. Quiere ofrecer un destino
luminoso y alegre, pero no es todo
y ustedes saben:
las sombras,
las sombras,
las sombras,
las sombras,
me molestan y no las puedo tolerar.

Hijitos míos, no hay que ponerse tristes
por cada triste despedida:
todas lo son, es sabido,
porque hay otra partida, otra cosa,
digamos,
donde nada,
nada
está resuelto.

Another Thing

Dear children, your father knows so little of you
and suffers for it. He wants to offer you a destiny
light-filled and happy, but that's not all
and you know:
the shadows,
the shadows,
the shadows,
the shadows
pester me and I cannot bear them.

My children, no need to be sad
at every sad goodbye:
they all are, that's well known,
because there's another departure, another thing,
we'll say,
where nothing,
nothing
is resolved.

Tu pequeño corazón

Apoya sobre mi brazo tu pequeño corazón. No temas, detrás de la ochava nada puede alarmarnos demasiado.

Sólo el horizonte que asoma para luego volver a esconderse.

Your Little Heart

Lay on my arm your little heart. Don't fear, behind the eighth
  nothing can alarm us too much.

Just the horizon that emerges only to hide itself.

Cánones

a Jorge Enrique Adoum

1

Cuidado con el calor
y el sabor; con
las esperanzas mal
paridas. Cuidado
con sonar
porque ha llegado el momento.

2

Claridad dueña
de vida y presagios.

Claridad rápida
y conmovida.

Sepulcro luminoso.

3

Dicen que se va
esta época
de amor
y desprecio.

Dicen que se va
su color, su fluido;

Canons

For Jorge Enrique Adoum

1

Careful with the heat
and the taste; with
hopes ill-
born. Careful
with dreaming
because the moment has come.

2

Clarity, owner
of life and premonitions.

Clarity, rapid
and poignant.

Brilliant tomb.

3

They say going
are the times
of love
and disdain.

They say going
is their color, their fluid;

se va, persiguiendo
certeza y mentiras. Saltando.

4

Apenas por venir. Ni siquiera volver
un poco: estaré
de ida siempre. De ida
miro, de ida caigo.

5

Tomaré este
destino compartido.

Sabré tocarlo
y descubrirlo;

masticar
y romper el olvido.

6

Un par de balazos en las polvaredas
que el sol parte; calles
rotas, sin orificio
de salida; agnósticas
y haraganas como el cristal, repartidas
en el ocaso, sangrando
en las oraciones, sacudidas
por el toque estrábico del Ángelus. Anídate:
es mi mejor

going, pursuing
certainty and lies. Leaping.

4

Scarcely arriving. Not even returning
a little: I will always
be going. Going
I watch, going I fall.

5

I will take
this shared destiny.

I will know to touch
and discover it;

to chew
and break forgetting.

6

A pair of gunshots in the dust clouds,
the sun parts: broken
streets, without an opening
to exit; agnostics
and wanderers like crystal, strewn
in the dawn, bleeding
in prayers, shaken
by the wall-eyed touch of the Angelus. Settle in:
this is my best

momento; ultramarino, fiando
sobre cada recelo.

7

Quién no ha pasado
por esta cintura de esperanza
y de prevención.

Por ese ecuador
más acá de los sacrificios.

moment; seafaring, trusting
above every suspicion.

7

Who hasn't passed
over this waist of hope
and prevention.

Over that equator
closer than sacrifices.

El nieto de Dios

Mi abuelo tenía un corazón bueno y algunos
gallos, competentes. Usaba un buen par de guardaespaldas
y un smoking, dos cadillacs, una sala
de juego –monte o baccarat– un casino en la margen
izquierda, sobre la ladera oriental y cansina
del macizo andino, al pie mismo de las nieves. También
un teatro de varieté donde las señoras bataclanas muestran
la liga, muestran el corset. Y mi abuelo banca
y se protégé merced a su "personal", diestro y siniestro.

La edad de mi abuelo andaría
por los ciento veinte años, un trozo considerable
de historia llena de sabor y dolor. Más
de un siglo de vida, si viviera rodeado de sus gallos
diestros, de su Lola Mora, la Bella
Otero de aquende los Pirineos, tapado por el frío
blanco de las drogas, de los armiños
abdicados, de redentores, de parroquianos; pilotos
y zepelines y volantas y vapores y peripecias
y ladinos de rara conversación y áspero
desdén por las garantías abiertas como alitas
de mariposas empotradas a galerazos.

Así, rodeado de cupletistas malsanas,
pero venturosas, vivió
y murió como la espuma deshecha
en el propio casino, sobre un manto de naipes, entre

The Grandson of God

My grandfather had a good heart and some
gamecocks, competent. He used a good pair of bodyguards
and a smoking jacket, two cadillacs, a game
room—monte or bacarat—a casino on the left
edge, over the eastern and weary side
of the Andean range, at the very feet of the snows. Also
a variety theater where the striptease girls show
their garters, show their corsets. And my grandfather banks
and plays it safe thanks to his "personnel," left and right.

My grandfather's age would be
around one hundred and twenty, a considerable bit
of history full of flavor and pain. More
than a century of life, if he had lived surrounded by his adept
chickens, by his Lola Mora, the Bella
Otero of this side of the Pyrenees, covered by the blank
cold of drugs, of squandered
ermines, of redeemers, of parishioners; pilots
and zeppelins and carriages and steamships and unforeseen turns
and ladinos with strange conversation and harsh disdain
for guarantees open like wings
of butterflies embedded in fedoras.

So, surrounded by cabaret singers sickly
though lucky, he lived
and died like foam diminished
in the casino itself, on a carpet of cards, through

picotazos diestros y sospechosos, o torvos simplemente. Vivió

y murió como la espuma deshecha
y la nieve; como las crestas de los gallos, los bailes
de las olas de mi buen abuelo: santificado
sea su nombre, vénganos en su reino, monarca
de los cielos bajos, de las nubes rastreras y luminosas.

Pepe Menese canta y las ostras
vuelan por su boca. El sabor
del mar llega hasta Chiclana de la Frontera y allí
va a enredarse en los tobillos sagrados de Antonio Farina.

El taconeo retumba, agrieta
el mundo como una queja carcelaria. Sacude
la memoria, agita
las llamas de los sufrimientos.

El mundo que grita de dolor
desde su celda, en el fondo
de las gargantas dispuestas.
Su olor es el sabor
del mar, el salto de la voz en guerra.

Cómo era tu piel interior, el mundo
terso, tu vida mía que volaba
con los reflejos, que velaba
sus arcabuces.

Hay que oír el grito oscuro

skilled, suspicious stings, or simply grim ones. He lived

and died like the diminished foam
and the snow; like the crests of the cocks, the dances
of the waves of my good grandfather: hallowed
be his name, his kingdom come, monarch
of the low skies, of the streaked and luminous clouds.

Pepe Menese sings and the oysters
fly through his mouth. The taste
of sea comes all the way to Chiclana de la Frontera and there
it will twist itself in the sacred ankles of Antonio Farina.

The footwork booms, the world
cracks like a prison break. Memory
whips, the flames
of suffering tremble.

The world shrieks in pain
from its cell, in the backs
of disposed throats.
Their scent is the taste
of sea, the leap of a voice at war.

What was your inner skin like, terse
world, your life of mine that flew
with the reflections, that watched over
its muzzle loaders.

The dark scream must be heard

y el sol nonato como tus amigos; hay
que ver los signos
de la antigua llama.

Estoy por abrir las puertas, por cerrar
los ojos y no mirar
más allá de mis narices, no oler,
no tocar el nombre de Dios en vano.

and the sun unborn like your friends; the signs
of the ancient flame
must be seen.

I am about to open the doors, to close
my eyes and not look
past my nostrils, not smell,
not touch the name of God in vain.

Peppermint

a Juan Gelman

a Juan Carlos Portantiero

no cantan
los que nunca conocieron una esperanza

dicen que la esperanza no aparece
y que algo se derrumba

dicen que se desliza la vida
por la pendiente donde comienza

que está en un declive
que se desploma por naturaleza
que la vida no es vida

no escuchan las risas que empujan al amanecer
ni el canto último del ebrio extenuado
que se aleja
abandonado la noche con indecisión

saben que caer es difícil
que después de los brindis
vienen los sueños y los presagios
que es penoso tranquilizar el corazón alegre
y el abandonado

Peppermint

For Juan Gelman
For Juan Carlos Portantiero

they don't sing
those who never knew hope

they say hope doesn't appear
and that something collapses

they say life slides
down the gradient it begins on

that it is in decline
that it tumbles by nature
that life isn't life

the laughter pushing at dawn doesn't listen
nor does the final song of the exhausted drunk
who moves on
abandoning the night to its indecision

they know that falling is difficult
that after the toasts
come dreams and predictions
that it is shameful to tranquilize a happy heart
and an abandoned one

nadie se atreve a cantar
junto al endurecido silencio
sin promesas

no one dares to sing
along with the hardened silence
without promises

Quiromancia

Hoy hace menos frío
que el año que viene, si viene. Vendrá
seguramente para que nadie
crea en las groserías de las profecías, o de los meros
sueños premonitorios. Esas tonterías
solferinas, esas fantasías sin importancia, tardes
en las que el corazón humano
se pone al rojo morado, se
diría. Se dirá, cuando haya
algo que decir: hoy
hace menos que el año que vendrá.

Palm Reading

Today it's less cold
than next year will be, if it comes. It will come
surely so that no one
can believe in the crudenesses of prophecies, or of mere
premonitory dreams. Those reddish-purple
idiocies, those unimportant fantasies, afternoons
in which the human heart
turns a purplish-red, you
could say. You will say, when there
is something to say: today
is less than next year will be.

Bar "La Calesita"

Es el fondo de un bar. Es un lugar parecido a una cueva donde uno se sienta, bebe y ve pasar a hombres enrarecidos por distintos problemas. Es una gran linterna mágica.

Es una gruta retirada del mundo que cobija a sus criaturas. Uno se siente allí ferozmente feliz.

Acaba de aparecer el primer hombre, apenas ha aprendido a caminar, aún no sabe defenderse.

El hombre sonríe y llora y sigue la fiesta.

Carousel Bar

It's the back of a bar. It's a place similar to a cave where one
sits, drinks, and watches men pass strained by different
troubles. It's a great magic lantern.

It's a den withdrawn from the world that shelters its creatures.
There, one feels fiercely happy.

The first man just appeared, has hardly learned to walk, still
cannot defend himself.

He smiles and cries and the festivities continue.

Quiero denunciar

Quiero denunciar ante todos, público
y clero, el robo de un par de anteojos, de alguna
camiseta sucia y pañuelo usado, un número
impreciso de poemas que venía escribiendo
en los últimos años de esta guerra, un aparato
de televisor, discos, armas, souvenires
varios: un libro de Lenin, un disco
de don Pepe de la Matrona que me regalara
el divino Divinsky por recomendación
del marqués del Cante, don Fernando
Quiñones, un asiento argelino, piedritas, cartas, dos botellas de
    vino
chileno, documentos reales y apócrifos y otras
cosas pequeñas pero queridas.
Nada de esto, ni de otras cosas que
omito han reaparecido. Fueron
robadas por la policía en mi domicilio, entonces
ilegal para ellos. Las armas perdidas ya
han sido debidamente detalladas, las largas
y las cortas, las buenas y las malas. Los
objetos eran comunes, como esos que se venden
por allí; los versos hablaban de una 11,25 que
ha dejado una marca en el nacimiento
del muslo izquierdo; otro hacía referencia
a los problemas de la balística en relación con
los sentimientos; uno recordaba el miedo
que tenía un sargento cuando

I Want to Report

I want to report before you all, public
and cleric, the theft of a pair of glasses, a few
dirtied t-shirts and used handkerchiefs, an imprecise
number of poems I had been working on
in the last years of this war, a television
set, albums, weapons, assorted
souvenirs: a book by Lenin, a record
by don Pepe de la Matrona
the divine Divinsky gave to me on recommendation
by the marquis of the Cante, don Fernando
Quiñones, an Algerian chair, decorative stones, letters, two
    bottles
of Chilean wine, real and apocryphal documents and other
things small but cherished.
None of this, nor of the other things
I omit has reappeared. It
was stolen by the police from my home, so,
illegally. The lost weapons have already
been duly described, the long
and the short, the good and the bad. The
objects were common, like those that are sold
around there; the verses discussed an 11.25mm that
has left a mark in the crease
of my left thigh; another referenced
the problems of ballistics in relation to
emotions; one recalled the fear
one sergeant showed when

fuera atacado por sorpresa, y otros
temas que he olvidado por buenas razones. Algunos de
estos papeles desaparecidos por el miedo que la policía
metió a mucha gente, entre ellas una mujer llamada
Lucila, que materialmente quemó uno que otro.
Otros fueron destruidos por la propia policía o los militares
de los servicios de informaciones que también
vinieron a buscarme y también me llevaron. Hago
esta denuncia,
especialmente por la pérdida
de armas y poemas, ya que ambos son irreparables. Han
sido robados al pueblo de la república, a
quien naturalmente pertenecían.

he was attacked by surprise, and other
topics that I've neglected for good reasons. Some of
these papers disappeared due to the fear that the police
instilled in many people, among them a woman named
Lucila, who materially burned them one by one.
Others were destroyed by the police themselves or the military
from information services who also
came to find me and also took me away. I file
this report,
especially for the loss
of weapons and poems, since both are unrecoverable. They
have been stolen from the people of the republic,
to whom they naturally belonged.

Autocrítica

La partida que vino a
buscarme tenía mucho
miedo pero no dio tiempo
a nada, a manotear una
sola arma.
Lástima que entre ellos no
había un solo Sargento Cruz,
sino más bien cobardes,
torturadores, violadores,
cada uno empuñaba una
buena arma larga.
Lástima de Cruz y lástima de
don Martín que tampoco
estaba.
No hay de qué quejarse,
entonces.

Self-Critique

The party that came
searching for me had a great
deal of fear but left no time
for anything, for grabbing a
single weapon.
Shame that among them there
wasn't a Sergeant Cruz,
only probably cowards,
torturers, rapists,
each one armed with one
great long weapon.
A shame about Cruz and a shame
about Don Martín who was also
not there.
No cause for complaint,
then.

La verdad es la única realidad

Del otro lado de la reja está la realidad, de
este lado de la reja también está
la realidad; la única irreal
es la reja; la libertad es real aunque no se sabe bien
si pertenece al mundo de los vivos, al
mundo de los muertos, al mundo de las
fantasías o al mundo de la vigilia, al de la explotación o de la
    producción.
Los sueños, sueños son; los recuerdos, aquel
cuerpo, ese vaso de vino, el amor y
las flaquezas del amor, por supuesto, forman
parte de la realidad; un disparo en
la noche, en la frente de estos hermanos, de estos hijos, aquellos
gritos irreales de dolor real de los torturados en
el ángelus eterno y siniestro en una brigada de policía
cualquiera
son parte de la memoria, no suponen necesariamente
el presente, pero pertenecen a la realidad. La única aparente
es la reja cuadriculando el cielo, el canto
perdido de un preso, ladrón o combatiente, la voz
fusilada, resucitada al tercer día en un vuelo inmenso cubriendo
    la Patagonia
porque las masacres, las redenciones, pertenecen a la realidad,
    como
la esperanza rescatada de la pólvora, de la inocencia
estival; son la realidad, como el coraje y la convalecencia
del miedo, ese aire que se resiste a volver después del peligro

Truth Is the Only Reality

On the other side of the bars is reality, on
this side of the bars is also
reality; the only unreal
thing is the bars: freedom is real even though it's not clear
whether it belongs to the world of the living, to
the world of the dead, to a fantasy
world or a world of vigilance, to one of exploitation or of
   production.
Dreams are dreams; memories, that
body, that glass of wine, love
and the frailties of love, of course, form
part of reality; a shot
fired in the night, in the forehead of these brothers, of these
   sons, those
unreal screams of real pain of the tortured in
the eternal and sinister Angelus of any police brigade
at all
are a part of memory, they don't necessarily mean
the present, but they belong to reality. The only apparent things
are the bars gridding the sky, the lost song
of an inmate, thief, or combatant, the executed
voice, resuscitated on the third day in an immense flight
   covering Patagonia
because the massacres, the redemptions, belong to reality, like
hope rescued from dust, from a summer
innocence: these are reality, like courage and the convalescence
of fear, that air that resists returning after danger

como los designios de todo un pueblo que marcha hacia la victoria
o hacia la muerte, que tropieza, que aprende a defenderse, a
    rescatar lo suyo, su
realidad.
Aunque parezca a veces una mentira, la única
mentira no es siquiera la traición, es
simplemente una reja que no pertenece a la realidad.

Cárcel de Villa Devoto, abril de 1973

like the plans of an entire people who march toward victory
or toward death, who stumble, who learn to defend themselves,
    to save their own, their
reality.
Though it seems sometimes to be real, the only
lie is not even betrayal, it's
simply these bars that don't belong to reality.

Villa Devoto Prison, April 1973

Mi tierra querida

Ya es hora de perder
la inocencia, ese
estupor de las criaturas que todavía
no pudieron hacerse cargo
de la memoria
del mundo al que recién nacieron.

Pero nosotros, hombres
grandes ya, podemos olvidar, sabemos
perfectamente qué tendríamos
que hacer para dañar
el presente, para romperlo.

Aquí nadie
tiene derecho a distraerse,
a estar asustado, a rozar
la indignación, a exclamar su sorpresa.

My Beloved Land

It's time to lose
innocence, that
stupor of the creatures that still
couldn't take hold
of the memory
of the world to which they were just born.

But we, men
older now, can forget, we know
perfectly what we would have to do
to damage
the present, to break it.

Here, no one
has the right to become distracted,
to be frightened, to feign
indignation, to exclaim their surprise.

El árbol de la vida

Una cisterna me ha descubierto
la cara del futuro. No hay bemoles
ni demonios más allá del agotamiento; ni figuras
consulares, ni ternura que vuele siquiera
como una transpiración sobre el horizonte luminoso.

Miro el pantano, la cisterna
que me rodea. La mirada
que no vislumbro, la acacia que no huelo: ay hijos
míos, cómo pensaba no quejarme, cómo
odiaba todo lamento; pero queja
y batalla suenan en la misma campana,

especialmente cuando miramos
el tiempo de derecha a izquierda, de adentro
hacía atrás y vuelan
los aires ambiguos, las luces
cruzadas del pecado de Alejandría.

The Tree of Life

A washbowl has shown me
the face of my future. There are no complications
or demons past my exhaustion; nor consular
figures, nor tenderness that floats, not even
as sweat over the lit horizon.

I look at the reservoir, the bowl
that surrounds me. That gaze
I can't catch, the acacia I can't smell: oh
my children, how I intended not to complain,
how I detested all laments; but complaint
and battle ring from the same bell,

especially when we look
at time from right to left, from inside it
facing back and ambiguous
airs fly, the crossed
lights of the sin of Alexandria.

El carterista

El moncho Angaco está
cosiendo laboriosamente dos
carteritas. Para
hacerlas, ha usado los pocos
elementos con que se cuenta en estas celdas
de Villa Devoto: un trabajo
de preso ducho, de hombre que
lleva casi dos años ya por esta
cárcel y también por Resistencia
y Rawson y el barco Granaderos que —ay—
dos compañeros oportunamente no pudieron volar. El
moncho Angaco es alto
fuerte y ágil como un siervo de Dios: un samurai
político y bondadoso; cuando cayó
tuvo mala suerte: se batió
o quiso batirse y la corredera
de la cuatro-cinco se trabó, o algo
por el estilo. Le han
pedido veintidós años de prisión que no
cumplirá porque hay
todo un pueblo que no quiere verlo tanto tiempo
encerrado porque hay un pueblo que lo quiere
mucho, aunque no lo vea coser
sus dos pequeñas carteras para sus hijitas,
aquí, en la celda cuarentaicinco de
Villa Devoto. Montonero Angaco: Viva
la Patria, Perón o muerte

The Purse Maker

The Angacan moncho is
laboriously sewing two
tiny purses. To
make them, he has used the few
materials to speak of in these cells
of Villa Devoto: the work
of a skilled inmate, of a man who
has spent almost two years now in this
prison and also in Resistencia
and Rawson and the Granaderos ship that—ay—
two compañeros fortuitously couldn't break. The
Angaco man is tall
strong and agile like a servant of God: a samurai
political and generous; when he fell
he had bad luck: he gave hell
or wanted to and the shutter
of the cuatro-cinco jammed,
or something along those lines. They have
asked of him twenty-two years imprisoned he won't
finish because there's
a whole town that doesn't want to see him put away
so long because there's a town that loves him
very much, even though they don't see him sew
his two tiny purses for his tiny daughters,
here, in the forty-fifth cell of
Villa Devoto. Montonero Angaco: Viva
la Patria, Perón or Death

y todo lo demás: queda
sellado así nuestro pacto
de sangre, nuestra suerte con
los que viajaban en esta
gran tierra de fuego y promesas
a conquistar, con toda
esa gente que no puede
mirarlo ahora, sino a través
de mis ojos inmerecidos, de sus
carteritas. Y que nadie
se atreva a dudar de mi
palabra inmerecida ni de los amores del pueblo
argentino, de su confianza, de su salud,
de sus juramentos, de sus brindis.

and all the rest: our pact
is sealed in
blood, our luck with
those who traveled in this
great world of fire and promises
of conquest, with all
those people who can't
see him now, only through
my undeserving eyes, his
little purses. May no one
dare to doubt my
undeserving word or the loves of the Argentine
people, their confidence, their health,
their judgments, what they choose to raise their glasses to.

Solicitada

Siempre los poetas fueron, en efecto, hombres
de transición, Roberto
Fernández Retamar; porque, realmente, si un poeta, amigo
mío, no ve las transiciones que saltan a su
alrededor como brotes de lava humeante, mejor
que deje de serlo, ceda ese guiso perfumado a otros olfatos
más perceptivos. Fue Baudelaire poeta
de transición y Talero; lo fueron el Ab-zul Agrib y Rosario
que cerraba los portales de las casas
de tolerancia; burdeles con quesos y vinos y jamones del
     diablo y
jarana agitando polleras y otros pabellones. Fueron
poetas de transición, los llantos y los crímenes en lugares
atroces y momentos inconvenientes; Dios mío, cuánta
poesía de transición fue grabada a cuchilla en la corteza
de las virginidades perdidas; cuánto baptisterio ha lamido
la sal de la transición, ha flameado
al son de los monaguillos: Giacopo de la Quercia fue hombre
de la transición, hasta la condesa
de Noailles debió escribir
poesía de transición. Y se me olvidan personas,
soplos que se esconden con los parches
transitorios, con los tránsitos de la gente desprevenida
que va despacito en busca de aguas y cielos
transitivos. Esos bostezos, esa gente,
son poemas de transición, mi querido Roberto; esas furias
en efecto, estas maneras violentas de caminar hacia el vacío: este

Solicited

Poets were always, effectively, men
of transition, Roberto
Fernández Retamar; because really, if a poet, my
friend, doesn't see the transitions leaping at his
sides like eruptions of smoking lava, better
that he ceases to be one, cedes that perfumed guise to other senses
more perceptive. Baudelaire was a poet
of transition, as was Talero; Ab-zul-Agrib and Rosario were
who closed the doors to the houses
of tolerance; brothels with cheeses and wines and hams of the
 devil and
the jarana rippling skirts and other flags. The cries and crimes
in atrocious places and untimely moments were poets
of transition; my God, how much
poetry of transition was engraved by blade in the rind
of lost virginities; how much baptistery has licked
the salt of transition, has fluttered
at the sound of altar boys: Jacopo della Quercia was a man
of the transition, even the countess
de Noailles must have written
poetry of transition. And I'm forgetting people,
leaks covered by transitory
patches, by the transiting of the unprepared masses
that go slowly in search of water and transitive
skies. Those yawns, those masses,
are poems of transition, my dear Roberto; those furies,
essentially, these violent methods of walking toward the void: this

tiempo siempre estuvo plagado; y si no hay
transiciones, habrá que señalar el fin de estos mundos
hostiles y movedizos, dar
los trompetazos y salir corriendo del campo de juego, entre
pedradas –seguramente– y pedorretas: será ese, a pesar
de todos los años de espera y anuncios, un dato bastante
    impopular;
una mala noticia, un poco tremendista como el mismo Apocalipsis.

En la superficie que salta
sobre la nieve, en la arruga
andina. Estrellado contra la firmeza
del cielo bajo, diluido
como un dios sin nombre, un aire
indirecto, un soplo vacío: emblemas
para ser escuchados y explicados; respondiendo
a preguntas y alegrías.

Averiguar en qué rincones anduvo
para dejar perecer todo este tiempo
sin que nadie soplara la ceniza del agua,
el arco de los ríos que no responden,
no articulan los hechos del tiempo efectuado.

En daños y muertes, cascotes testigos
de la iniquidad, sangre disparada, quemarropas
a traición –pienso en José, por ejemplo, en su
bondad luminosa, en el derecho de su esperanza–, vengo
a caer sobre el lomo
de estas últimas

time was always plagued; and if there are no
transitions, it will be necessary to signal the end of these hostile
and restless worlds, sound
the trumpets and leave running from the playing field, beneath
the thrown rocks—surely—and blown raspberries: it will be,
   despite
all the years of waiting and warning, a fairly unpopular fact;
a piece of bad news, a little alarmist, like the Apocalypse itself.

On the surface that leaps
over the snow, on the Andean
crease. Starry against the firmness
of the low sky, diluted
like a nameless god, an indirect
air, an empty breeze: emblems
to be heard and explained; responding
to questions and happinesses.

Verify the corners in which it went
to perish this whole time
without anyone blowing the ash off the water,
the arc of the rivers that don't respond,
don't articulate the acts of completed time.

In harms and deaths, cast-off witnesses
of injustice, blood spread, point-blank
treason—I'm thinking of José, for example, of his
luminous goodness, of the right he had to hope—, I come
to fall over the back
of these last

palabras reunidas para ser resueltas.

Una sola ráfaga del tiempo pasado,
pronunciada sílaba por sílaba, acto por acto. En
el revuelo, debajo de los primeros terrones,
vengo a ofrecer la inutilidad
de mi derrota, abrir el desquite
sobre la muerte (esa pre-dicción, gritar)
una victoria abierta como el pasado que vendrá
como mi vida que no me pertenece
en tanto que es ajena —otros se han apropiado, a
otros se la debo— y común al grueso del destino.

Esa memoria, concertadora de las personas, esa
signadora del porvenir que espera con los brazos
abiertos; esta vida que salta sobre mis espaldas
para seguir su juego y su rango. Deja
atrás la fatalidad enterrada también, como los virreyes,
como el egoismo insepulto, conjurado
en la soledad, porque la vida —lo he visto— depende
de un hilo conductor y generoso, cierra
los circuitos cortos, ovala los huevos inútiles.

En las criaturas del sol que salta, la maravilla
que esconde las uñas, acaricio
a los animales preferidos del universo intacto, el
esplendor de la piel del metal
que suelta los truenos de la imaginación, los alimentos
devorados por la buena ventura.

words reunited to be resolved.

One single gust of time past,
pronounced syllable by syllable, act by act. In
the commotion, beneath the first clods,
I come to offer the uselessness
of my defeat, to open revenge
over death (that pre-speech, the scream),
a victory wide like the past that will come forth
like my life which doesn't belong to me
as long as it's foreign—others have appropriated, to
others I owe it—and common to the majority of destiny.

That memory, arranger of people, that
signer of the future that waits with arms
open; this life that leaps over my shoulders
to continue its game and its rank. It leaves
behind fatality also buried, like the viceroys,
like disinterred egoism, conjured
in loneliness, because life—I have seen it—depends
on a conductive and generous wire, closes
the short circuits, makes ovals from imperfect eggs.

In the creatures of the sun that rises, the marvel
that hides claws, I caress
the favorite animals of the intact universe, the
splendor of the metal skin
that releases the roar of the imagination, the sustenances
devoured by good fortune.

Y la historia de la alegría no será
privativa, sino de toda la pendencia
de la tierra y su aire, su espalda y su perfil, su tos y su risa. Ya no
   soy
de aquí; apenas me siento una memoria
de paso. Mi confianza se apoya en el profundo desprecio
por este mundo desgraciado. Le daré
la vida para que nada siga como está.

And the history of happiness will not
be exclusive, but belong to all of the quarrelling
earth and its air, its back and its profile, its cough and its laugh.
    I am no longer
from here; I hardly feel I am a memory
in passing. My confidence balances on a profound disdain
for this disgraceful world. I will give
my life so that nothing continues as it is.

El ocaso de los dioses

No hay nadie en la calle, en los ruidos húmedos, en el vuelo
de las hojas y mis pasos quieren reiniciar las maderas de la
adolescencia.

Pero todo está abandonado, no hay nada que pueda
favorecernos; ningún aire de inconsciencia, ningún reino
de libertad. Sólo hábitos tolerantes haciendo crujir nuestra
memoria. "Ha estado bien", decimos.

Dueños de incendio, de la bondad del crepúsculo, de nuestro hacer,
de nuestra música, del único amor incoherente; soberanos de esa
calle donde los tactos y la impresión hicieron su universo.

Las sombras acarician aún sus veredas, tu mismo nombre y tu
gesto son una forma nocturna que en esa constelación crece y
sabe enrostrar nuestra culpa.

Y todo termina con una esperanza, con una dilación −"ha
estado bien"−, o en un bostezo, o en otro lugar donde es
menester el coraje.

The Decline of the Gods

There's no one in the street, its humid sounds, in the flight
of leaves and my steps want to start again on the rungs of
adolescence.

But everything is abandoned, there is nothing here that would
side with us; no unconscious air, no reign of liberty. Only
tolerant habits grinding down our memories. "It has been
good," we said.

Rulers of fire, of the goodness of dawn, of our making, of our
music, of the only incoherent love; sovereign of that street
where touches and impressions made their universe.

The shadows still caress the sidewalks, your own name and
gesture are a nocturnal form in that constellation and it grows
and is able to put a face to our guilt.

And everything ends with a hope, with a delay—"it has been
good"—, or in a yawn, or in another place where courage is
imperative.

Fuego nocturno

Los sueños dejan ver las libres gaviotas. Es con el hueso de tus ojos, es tu corazón que arde, atrás con los pajonales.

Y luego la calma chica, el aire enrarecido y el deseo de volver a vivir.

Nocturnal Fire

Dreams let the free gulls be visible. With the bone of your eyes,
  it's your heart that burns, behind among the scrublands.

And then a brief calm, the charged air, and the desire to live
  again.

Mensaje cifrado

Sólo te pido que dejemos este parque, que abandonemos sus
   municiones, sus reproches para irnos por ahí, como cascaritas
divertidas de pálidos carnavales; hielo y materia de olvido.
   Porque
entre tirones y sufrimientos, la cosa se ha puesto
tan fácil, tan fácil, que nadie
puede resolver sus entusiasmos, ordenar sus festejos.

Encoded Message

All I ask you is that we leave this park, abandon its munitions,
   its reproaches for our going there, like silly
masks at paled carnivals: the ice and the material of forgetting.
   Because
between strain and suffering, the matter has become
so easy, so easy, that no one
can solve its enthusiasms, arrange its festivities.

Muchas gracias

Sirve y me inclino
ante tu palabra, luz de mi pensamiento. Abrirán
las puertas, dejarán entender: los artistas, los
intelectuales, siempre
han sacudido el polvo de la realidad; descubrieron
caminos, emancipaciones
que no siempre lograron recorrer: era
prematuro en algunos casos, en otros fue distinto
—convengamos—, otras palabras son, bajar
la corredera de la mira, buscar con el guión
y dar justamente sobre algo que puede
moverse; un bulto,
un meneo a menos de cien metros
de tu corazón vulnerable, también enemigo.

*

La suerte ha dejado aquí de andar
fallando: se encendió la luz y pudo verse el caos, las
flagrancias: esa mano
allí, esta codicia; el miedo y otras mezquindades se pusieron
en evidencia y el amor
no aparecía por ninguna parte. Recompuestos
de la sorpresa, rendidos ante los hechos, nadie
pudo negar que en este país, en este
continente, nos estamos todos muriendo de vergüenza.

*

Thank You Very Much

Serve and I'll bend
before your word, light for my thought. They'll open
the doors, they'll make it known, the artists, the
intellectuals, have
always shaken the dust off reality; discovered
ways, emancipations
that they couldn't always traverse; they were
premature in some cases, in others it was different
—we'll agree—, those are other words, lowering
the shaft of the sight, using the guides
to set on something that could
move; a shape,
a rustling less than a hundred meters
from your vulnerable heart, also enemy.

    *

Here, luck has ceased to go on
failing; the light was lit and chaos could be seen, the
flagrancies: that hand
there, this greed; fear and other malignancies became
evidence and love
did not appear anywhere. Remade
from surprise, rent from what happened, no one
could deny that in this country, in this
continent, we are all dying of shame.

    *

Aquí estoy perdiendo amigos, buscando
viejos compañeros de armas, ganándome tardíamente
la vida, queriendo respirar
trozos de esperanzas, bocanadas de aliento; salir
volando para no hacer agua, para
ver toda la tierra y caer en sus brazos.

Here I am losing friends, looking
for old comrades-in-arms, gaining life
late, wanting to breathe in
fragments of hope, mouthfuls of breath; to leave
flying to avoid floundering, to
see the whole earth and fall in its arms.

CPSIA information can be obtained
at www.ICGtesting.com
Printed in the USA
FSHW011734170119
55066FS